Incredible Molluscs

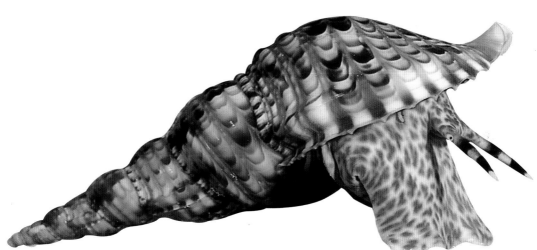

EXPRESS EDITION

John Townsend

www.raintreepublishers.co.uk
Visit our website to find out more information about **Raintree** books.

To order:
☎ Phone 44 (0) 1865 888113
▤ Send a fax to 44 (0) 1865 314091
▭ Visit the Raintree Bookshop at **www.raintreepublishers.co.uk** to browse our
catalogue and order online.

First published in Great Britain by Raintree Publishers,
Halley Court, Jordan Hill, Oxford, OX2 8EJ,
part of Harcourt Education Ltd.
Raintree is a registered trademark of Harcourt
Education Ltd.

Produced for Raintree Publishers by Discovery Books Ltd
Editorial: Louise Galpine, Sarah Jameson,
Charlotte Guillain, and Diyan Leake
Expert Reader: Jill Bailey
Design: Victoria Bevan, Keith Williams (sprout.uk.com
Limited), and Michelle Lisseter
Picture Research: Maria Joannou
Production: Duncan Gilbert and Jonathan Smith
Printed and bound in China by South China
Printing Company
Originated by Repro Multi Warna

ISBN 1 844 43452 4 (hardback)
09 08 07 06 05
10 9 8 7 6 5 4 3 2 1

ISBN 1 844 43472 9 (paperback)
09 08 07 06 05
10 9 8 7 6 5 4 3 2 1

British Library Cataloguing in Publication Data
Townsend, John
Incredible Molluscs. – (Incredible Creatures)
594
A full catalogue record for this book is available from the
British Library.

This levelled text is a version of Freestyle:
Incredible creatures: Incredible molluscs.

Photo acknowledgements
Alamy Images p. 12 left (IMAGINA/Atsushi Tsunoda);
Christine Osborne World Religions p. 38 left; Corbis pp. 4
(Todd A. Gipstein), 14 left (Stuart Westmorland), 36 right
(Stuart Westmorland), 47 right (Peter Steiner), 48 (Paul A.
Souders), 49 left (Araldo de Luca); FLPA pp. 5 left (F.
Bavendam), 6 left (Roger Wilmshurst), 8–9 (D. P. Wilson),
10–11 (F. Bavendam), 11 right (F. Lanting), 12–13 (A.
Wharton), 14–15 (Michael Rose), 16 left (Michael Rose), 18
inset (D. P. Wilson), 18 main (Peter David), 23 left (Gerard
Lacz), 23 right (Tony Hamblin), 26 bottom (F. Bavendam),
30–1 (Derek Middleton), 31 right (Colin Marshall), 32–3 (B.
Cranston), 46 left (Martin Witherg); Hawaii Photo Resource
pp. 20–1 (Jack Jeffrey); Imagequest 3-D p. 28 left (James D.
Watt); Mary Evans Picture Library p. 41 right; Nature
Photographers p. 49 right; Nature Picture Library pp. 10 left
(B. Jones & M. Shimlock), 22 (Jason Smalley), 25 right
(Dietmar Nill), 29 right (Constantinos Petrinos), 28–9 (Jeff
Rotman), 38–9 (Jeff Rotman); NHPA pp. 5 top (Lawrence
Lawry), 5 middle (Karl Switak), 5 bottom (G. I. Bernard), 6–7
(Laurie Campbell), 7 right (Roy Waller), 9 right (E.A. Janes),
13 right (Pete Atkinson), 15 right (Matt Bain), 16–17 (Laurie
Campbell), 17 right, 20 left (Daniel Heuclin), 26 top (Image
Quest 3-D), 27 (Norbert Wu), 33 right (Norbert Wu), 34 left
(B. Jones & M. Shimlock), 35 right (James Carmichael Jr), 40
top (ANT Photo Library), 40–1 (Norbert Wu), 42 (Lawrence
Lawry), 43 top (ANT Photo Library), 44 top (Image Quest 3-
D), 44–5 (Karl Switak), 46–7 (G. I. Bernard); Oxford Scientific
Films pp. 8 left (John McCammon), 30 left, 32 left (Karen
Gowlett-Holmes), 39 right (Howard Hall); Science Photo
Library pp. 19 (Mauro Fermariello), 21 right (Clouds Hill
Imaging Ltd), 24 (Peter Scoones), 25 left (Sinclair Stammers),
34–5 (Matthew Oldfield), 36 left (Jon Wilson), 37 (Georgette
Duowma), 43 bottom, 50 (Ron Church), 51 (Tim Beddow);
USDA p. 45 right (Aphis). Cover photograph of a Roman
snail reproduced with permission of Premaphotos Wildlife
(Ken Preston-Mafham).

The Publishers would like to thank Jon Pearce for his
assistance in the preparation of this book. Every effort has
been made to contact copyright holders of any material
reproduced in this book. Any omissions will be rectified in
subsequent printings if notice is given to the Publishers.

Contents

Any words appearing in the text in bold, **like this**, are explained in the Glossary. You can also look out for some of them in the 'Wild words' bank at the bottom of each page.

The world of molluscs

Would you believe it?

Scientists think molluscs were one of the earliest forms of life on Earth, over 550 million years ago.

For thousands of years, humans have used molluscs for food, money, and jewellery.

Did you know that molluscs live all around us? There may be over 100,000 different types or **species** of mollusc on Earth. Most of them move around rather slowly.

Most molluscs live in the sea. Others live in streams or on dry land. You can find molluscs in deserts and mountains. You can also find molluscs in your garden or local park.

▶ Mollusc shells make good musical instruments! This shell is from a trumpet conch.

▲ Octopuses are a kind of mollusc. They have long **tentacles** around their mouths.

Find out later ...

... how an oyster makes pearls.

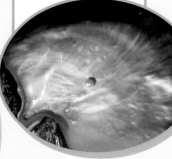

... what is the world's biggest land snail.

... why mollusc slime is important.

What is a mollusc?

Molluscs are **invertebrates**. This means they have no backbone. The word mollusc means soft. They have soft bodies, so many molluscs use hard shells for protection.

There are three main groups of molluscs:

- Snails and slugs (**gastropods**)
- Mussels, clams, and oysters (**bivalves**)
- Squid, octopuses, and cuttlefish (**cephalopods**).

tentacle part of an animal that looks like a long, thin, bendy arm

Meet the family

Each group of molluscs has some pretty amazing members.

Slugs and snails

Slugs and snails are the best known **gastropods**. They move along slowly on their soft belly, which acts like a big, slimy foot.

Slugs and snails on land usually like to live in cool, damp places under rocks and leaves. Sea slugs and snails are often very brightly coloured.

Slug or snail?

Slugs are like snails without shells, but some slugs have tiny shells under their skin to protect their soft bodies.

▼ This great grey slug moves along the ground on its belly.

Wild words   gastropod mollusc that moves along on its soft belly

Limpets and periwinkles

Have you seen limpets at the seaside clinging tightly to rocks when the tide goes out? They have a strong, **muscular** foot. The foot clamps on to the rock so nothing can remove them.

Periwinkles are sea snails that live on seashores. When hiding in their shell, they block up the entrance with a hard plate like a little door. This keeps them safe inside.

Whelks

Whelks like to eat other molluscs. They use their long, sharp tongue to drill into the shells of oysters and mussels. Then they slurp up the soft insides like a milkshake!

◄ This rock pool is full of periwinkles. Can you spot the limpet among them?

muscular has strong muscles

Bivalves

Bivalve molluscs live in water. They have two shells joined by a **hinge**. Bivalves open their shells to sift tiny pieces of food from the water. Mussels, clams, and oysters are bivalves. We eat them as seafood.

Oysters and clams

Oysters often live in groups, called oyster beds. The giant clam is the largest bivalve and can grow up to 1 metre (3 feet) across. That is at least three times bigger than your dinner plate!

Boat wreckers!

Shipworms (shown below) are clams that make holes in wood. They can drill a tunnel through a thick wooden plank in less than one year. They can do a lot of damage to wooden boats.

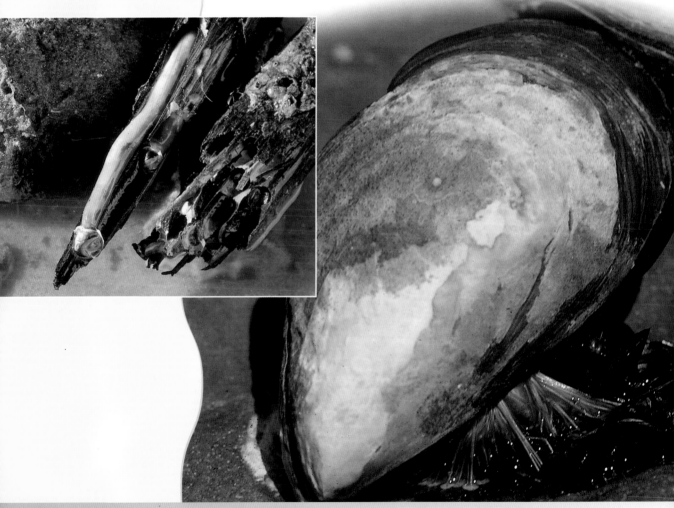

hinge joint that moves, like the part that fixes a door to a frame and allows it to open and close

Mussels

There are many different types of mussel. They cling hard to rocks using strong, sticky threads on their **muscular** foot.

Scallops and cockles

Scallops and **cockles** live partly buried in sand or mud. Unlike most other bivalves, scallops can swim.

Bird dangers

Birds like this oystercatcher eat molluscs. They can break open the shells of mussels and oysters with their hard beaks. Then they scoop out the soft centre.

◄Can you see the thin, sticky threads holding these mussels on to the rock?

The cephalopods

Octopus, squid, and cuttlefish are types of **cephalopod**. They are different from other molluscs. Most have no outside shell and some can move very fast. They have long **tentacles** around their mouths.

Octopus and squid

Many octopus and squid live deep in the ocean. The giant squid is the largest **invertebrate** on Earth.

Many arms

All octopuses have eight tentacles. Squid and cuttlefish (shown above) have ten. If an octopus loses a tentacle in a fight, it can grow a new one!

▶ This is a Maori octopus. It lives in the sea off the coast of Australia.

tentacle part of an animal that looks like a long, thin, bendy arm

Cuttlefish

Cuttlefish look like small, flat squid. They have a shell-like bone inside their bodies. Sometimes you can find these white shells washed up on beaches.

Nautilus

The nautilus is the only type of cephalopod that has an outside shell like other molluscs. It can also have up to 90 tentacles. It swims along the seabed to find its food.

A tough life

Sharks, penguins, seals, whales, and humans all like to eat cephalopods. If they do not get eaten, octopuses can live for three years. Giant squid and giant octopuses can reach five years old.

▼ This seabird is feeding its chick on some squid.

Shell shapes

Mollusc shells come in all shapes, sizes, and colours. Many are very beautiful. A gastropod shell can look like a cap, an ear, or a corkscrew. A bivalve shell can be shaped like a frisbee or a fan.

Odds and ends

As well as **gastropods, bivalves,** and **cephalopods,** there are other types of mollusc.

Armour-plated

Chitons, or coat-of-mail shells, have shells that look like suits of armour. They live in the sea and in rock pools. Like limpets, they can stick hard to rocks. They feed on plants called **algae**. Chitons have no eyes.

▲ Like the limpet on the right, the chiton (above) can stick fast to rocks.

algae type of plant without stems that grows in water or on rocks

Bottoms up

Tusk shells live head down in the sand. Their shells stick up like elephant tusks. They use their **tentacles** to feed in the sand.

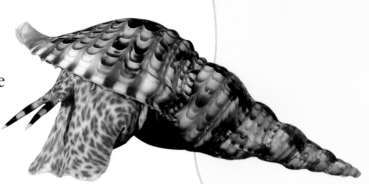

Weird molluscs

Some molluscs even look like worms. They have no shell and no eyes. They live deep down in the ocean and spend their days creeping over the seabed.

▲ This is a triton trumpet snail. It is a sea snail and can grow to a length of 30 centimetres (12 inches).

Long and short

The largest molluscs belong to the cephalopod family.

Giant squid can be up to 20 metres (over 65 feet) long. That is the length of more than five cars! The smallest squid is smaller than your big thumbnail.

Amazing bodies

Walkabout

Some **species** of octopus, such as the Caribbean reef octopus (below), can leave the water to hunt for food in rock pools. They cannot stay out of the water for more than a few minutes because they are not able to breathe on land.

Molluscs have amazing bodies that allow them to live in very difficult conditions.

Speedy molluscs

The fastest molluscs are squid. They can swim fast by letting water into their bodies and squirting it out again at high speed. This drives them forward through the water.

Cuttlefish glide through the water. They can move up and down by changing the amount of liquid or air inside their bones.

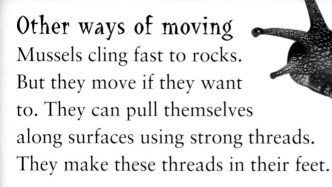

Other ways of moving

Mussels cling fast to rocks. But they move if they want to. They can pull themselves along surfaces using strong threads. They make these threads in their feet.

Cockles jump along the seabed using their **muscular** foot. **Scallops** swim by slamming shut their two shells. This forces out water and they jerk along.

As slow as a snail

The common garden snail, like this one, takes more than three minutes to move 1 metre (3 feet).

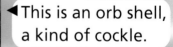

◀ This is an orb shell, a kind of cockle.

Breathing on land

Land slugs and snails do not have gills like water molluscs. Instead, they breathe through a small hole in the side of their head. They can also take in oxygen through their wet skin.

Breathing

All animals need **oxygen** to live. They breathe by taking in oxygen from air or water. The animal's blood then carries oxygen to the brain and muscles where it is needed.

Land animals, like us, have lungs. Water molluscs and many small water animals can breathe under water. They take in oxygen using little flaps called **gills**.

▲ Mussels take in food, as well as oxygen, through their gills. The gills on this mussel look like lots of little fingers.

oxygen one of the gases in air and water that all living things need

High and dry

Sea molluscs fan water over their gills to breathe. Some molluscs have special holes for the water to go in and out of their shell.

When the tide goes out, sea molluscs like limpets are left out of water. So how do they breathe? They trap a tiny puddle of water in their shell.

Slow breathing

Like most water molluscs, the periwinkles below can slow down their breathing when they are out of water. They can **survive** without oxygen until the tide comes back in.

▲ These molluscs have trapped a small amount of water in their shells so they can breathe when the tide goes out.

gills delicate, feathery structures that allow some animals to breathe under water

17

Eyes everywhere

Some **scallops** have lots and lots of eyes. They help the scallop look out for **predators**. Look closely at the scallop below. Can you see the two rows of little black eyes?

Sight

Most molluscs cannot see very well. However, **cephalopods** like squid and octopuses have good vision. Their eyes are similar to human eyes. Like us, they can turn their eyes to look in different directions.

The giant squid has the largest eyes in the animal kingdom. The eye of a giant squid is over 120 times bigger than a human eye!

▲ For the size of its head, a squid's eyes are enormous.

predator animal that kills and eats other animals

Touch and smell

An octopus has a very good sense of touch. It has lots of suckers on its **tentacles** that are used for touching and tasting. The suckers also help the octopus to hold on to its food.

Some **gastropods** have a well-developed sense of smell. They can sniff out food in the water from some distance away.

▼ Can you see the whitish suckers on the tentacles of this octopus?

Feeding

Growing a shell

Many molluscs have outer shells. They grow their shells by taking in **calcium** from the food they eat. Tiny shells and bones contain a lot of calcium. Our teeth also contain calcium.

Like most animals, molluscs spend a lot of time finding and eating food. Eating gets **nutrients** into their bodies. Nutrients are needed to give the body energy and help it grow.

Some molluscs eat plants and some eat other animals. Different types of mollusc have different ways of finding their food and eating it.

▼ This is a wolf snail. It is eating a smaller snail.

nutrient substance found in food that is needed by the body to grow strong and healthy

The right tool for the job

Many molluscs have a special tongue called a **radula**. It is long and rough and covered with tiny teeth. The radula is just right for poking into other shells or scraping **algae** from rocks.

Bivalves, like mussels and oysters, do not have a radula. They use their **gills** for breathing and to trap food. Little hairs on the gills move tiny pieces of food towards the mouth.

Breaking into shells

This photograph shows the radula of a mollusc very close up. You can see the rows of tiny, sharp teeth quite clearly. Only molluscs have a tongue like this.

algae type of plant without stems that grows in water or on rocks

Herbivores

Some molluscs are **herbivores**. This means they eat plants. **Chitons** eat plants called **algae** that grow on rocks under the water.

Plant-eaters

On land, many molluscs eat plants. Land slugs hide away in the daytime. They come out at night when it is dark and damp to munch the plants in our gardens. They can be a pest on farms because they feed on many fruits and vegetables.

Plants contain many good **nutrients**. Special juices in the mollusc's stomach break down food so the nutrients can get into the blood.

▼ This slug is eating a juicy, green leaf.

chiton ('ky-ton') mollusc with an oval shell made up of eight overlapping plates

Lots of teeth

A slug's **radula** can have up to 27,000 tiny teeth!
Like sharks, slugs lose and re-grow their teeth
throughout their lives. No wonder they are
such a nuisance in our gardens!

Slugs and snails are also food
for other animals.
Birds, badgers, and
hedgehogs all like
a tasty slug or
snail to eat.

▶ These are common
snails. They can
quickly destroy
a plant.

Beer traps

Some gardeners
make traps for
land slugs and
snails using jam
jars of beer.
Molluscs love the
sweet smell and
fall into the trap.
Because they do
not have **gills**
like sea molluscs,
they drown.

radula tongue that is long and rough

Hunters

Many sea molluscs are **carnivores**. This means they hunt and feed on smaller animals, such as other molluscs, fish, or fish eggs.

Cephalopods such as octopuses and squid catch fish and crabs. Their **tentacles** have little suckers to help them grip slippery food. These molluscs have strong jaws to tear up food. Their jaws are shaped like beaks.

Underwater vampire

One type of sea snail is called the vampire snail. It feeds on the blood of sleeping parrot fish. It clings on near the fish's mouth and eats its blood.

▲ This sea snail is feeding on coral. Although it may not kill the coral, it will probably damage it.

24   Wild words   coral tiny sea animals that use rings of tentacles for feeding. Many have hard outer bodies.

Clever tricks

Octopuses often attract their **prey** by wiggling the tip of a tentacle so it looks like a worm in the sand. They poison their prey with a bite.

Parasites

Some molluscs are **parasites**. This means they feed on other living animals without killing them. Sea snails feed on **coral** and starfish in this way.

▼ This is the beak of a giant squid. It is very sharp, to kill other sea animals.

Egg shell

Some fish, like this bitterling above, make use of mussels. The fish lays its eggs inside the shell of the common pond mussel. The tiny fish hatch and grow safe inside the mussel shell. Then after a few weeks, they swim away.

prey animal that is killed and eaten by other animals

Breeding

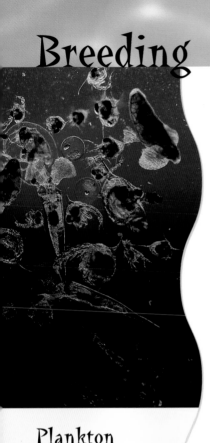

Molluscs have lots of different ways of making new molluscs.

Meeting up

Molluscs do not make any sounds. Instead, they use their eyes and sense of smell to meet up.

Land snails and slugs follow slime trails to find each other. Squid and cuttlefish turn bright colours to catch the eye of a partner.

Plankton

The tiny plants and animals that drift about in the sea are called **plankton**. They are food for many sea animals. Mollusc eggs are plankton.

▼ This cuttlefish wants to find a partner. It is showing off its beautiful colours and patterns.

mate when a male and female animal come together to produce young

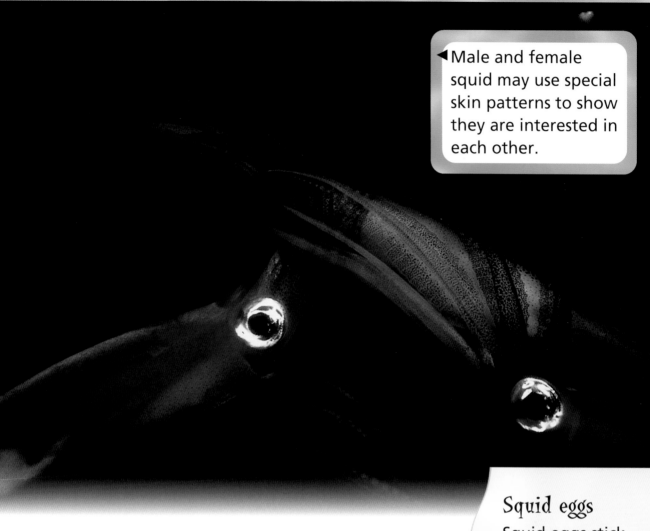

Male and female squid may use special skin patterns to show they are interested in each other.

Mating cuttlefish

Male and female cuttlefish lock their **tentacles** together to **mate**. After mating, the female lays up to 200 sticky, white eggs.

Tiny cuttlefish hatch out after four months. They are about the length of a paper clip. Many of them are eaten by **predators**. It is a dangerous time for a young cuttlefish.

Squid eggs

Squid eggs stick to seaweed or to the seabed. Some squid lay their eggs in the deep sea. These eggs drift around in the dark water. Many are eaten by fish.

Egg dangers

Very few mollusc eggs grow up into adults. This is because lots of animals eat them when they are tiny eggs or **plankton**. This manta ray is feeding on plankton. Look how big its mouth is!

Getting together

Octopuses live alone except when it is time to **mate**. When a male octopus wants to mate, he puts on a show of changing colours. He will often fight other male octopuses for the female. After mating, the female octopus swims off to find a safe, rocky den to lay her eggs.

▶ These **coral** are feeding on a young octopus. Many young octopuses die before they become adults.

plankton tiny plants and animals that drift about in the sea

Octopus eggs

A female octopus can lay 150,000 eggs in around two weeks. She attaches the eggs to the roof of her den like bunches of grapes. She guards them and keeps them clean. When they are ready to hatch, she helps her young to escape from their eggs. When this is done, she dies.

Egg champion

The giant clam, shown below, can release an amazing 1000 million eggs in one go. Most clam eggs are eaten before they can hatch.

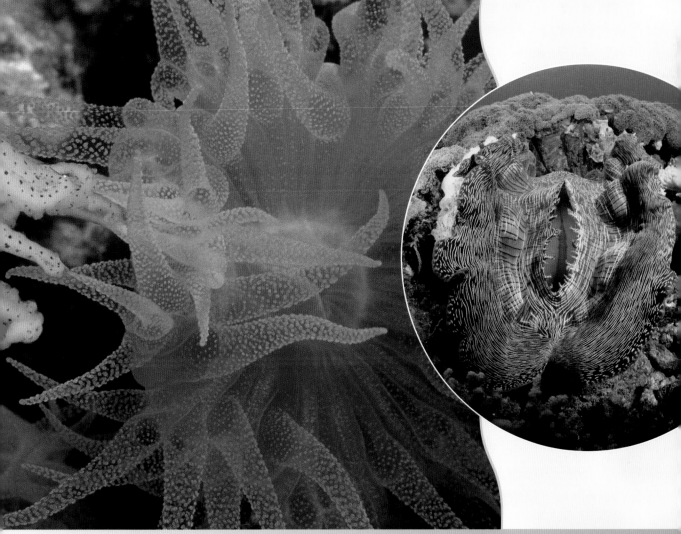

How oysters make young

The European oyster does not need to worry about meeting another oyster to **mate** with. It can make young oysters all on its own.

Bluepoint oysters have a different method. Females lay millions of eggs in the water. The eggs hatch into wriggly **larvae**. They swim around for two or three weeks. Then they settle among the stones and gravel and begin to grow.

Growing in the gills

Eggs of the common European oyster develop in the mother oyster's gills. Here, they are safe from fish and other predators.

larva (more than one are called larvae) young form of an animal that is very different from the adult

Hitching a ride

The larvae of mussels live in rivers. They grow in their mother's **gills**. When a trout swims by, the mussel releases her young. They float up to the fish and cling on with little hooks.

The larvae live in the gills of trout and feed there for a month or two. They grow there, safe from **predators**.

Life and death

Cuttlefish are able to **breed** by the time they are two years old. After laying their eggs (shown above), the females lose strength and their bodies quickly close down. Their lives soon end and they never see their own young grow up.

◄This is a brown trout. It might be carrying lots of mussel larvae around in its gills.

Defence

Hide and seek

One way to escape predators is to hide from them. Some molluscs bury themselves in the sand. They cover themselves with small shells and bits of **coral** so they are hard to see.

Very few molluscs grow old. They have soft, juicy bodies and they are tasty to eat. But many molluscs have ways of protecting themselves.

Coloured bodies

Many **cephalopods** can change the colour and patterns on their skin. This helps them to blend in with their surroundings. It makes it harder for **predators** to see them.

▲ A king **scallop** buries itself in pebbles and sand to hide from predators.

cephalopod ('sef-a-la-pod') mollusc that has tentacles around its mouth

All change

A cuttlefish can change colour in an instant. If put on top of different patterns such as straight lines or zig zags, a cuttlefish can copy the design exactly. This means it can hide from predators.

Many squid can glow in different colours. This may help to confuse animals that want to attack them.

Brilliant colours

Some sea slugs are very brightly coloured. This is a Spanish dancer. It turns bright red when it thinks it is in danger. Bright colours may stop predators from chasing it.

◀ This reef squid can go from bright red to green in the blink of an eye.

Beware!

Blue-ringed octopuses live in rock pools around the coast of Australia. They are small but deadly. If frightened or teased they can bite a human even through a wetsuit.

The poison in their bite is incredibly strong. Just one of these octopuses could kill up to 26 humans in a very short time.

Pretty poisonous

Bright colours are often a warning to **predators** that the animal is bad to eat. The red and yellow colours of this sea slug below warn that it is poisonous.

　　predator　animal that kills and eats other animals

Deadly bite

If bitten by a blue-ringed octopus you may feel nothing at first. But after a few minutes you will feel sick and dizzy. Then you lose your eyesight. After another minute or two you cannot move and will find it hard to breathe.

The only hope is to get to a doctor immediately.

Deadly shells

Cone shells (see above) have a deadly weapon. They have tiny teeth like little darts, which they fire at their **prey**. The darts are poisonous and can even kill humans.

◀ This is a blue-ringed octopus. The blue rings appear when it is about to attack.

prey animal that is killed and eaten by other animals

Special tricks

Many **cephalopods** have an unusual trick to help them escape from **predators**. They squirt out jets of black ink. This makes a dark cloud in the water and can confuse a predator. It gives the mollusc time to make a quick escape. Octopuses, squid, and cuttlefish use this method to escape from a predator.

Armour

Molluscs with shells can hide in them when danger comes. Some, like the sea snail above, have spiky shells. Some have spikes and teeth at the entrance of their shell to keep predators out.

▶ A giant octopus squirts out a cloud of ink to keep a diver away.

▲ This octopus is making itself look like a fierce lionfish.

A clever actor

The **mimic** octopus is a clever copycat. It can turn itself into the shape of other dangerous animals. It copies, or mimics, the shape of the banded sea snake by hiding six of its **tentacles** in the sand. It waves the other two about so it looks like a snake. This helps to put off predators.

Breathe in

Octopuses can squeeze themselves into very tiny gaps in the rocks. This is because they have soft bodies. It is a very useful way of escaping danger.

mimic (noun) one living thing that can copy another living thing

Weird and wonderful

Some molluscs grow to enormous sizes and are amazing animals.

Giant octopuses

The giant octopus is the largest **species** of octopus in the world. One of the largest known was caught off the coast of New Zealand in 2002. It weighed about as much as an adult human.

Disappearing giant

Unfortunately, giant clams (see below) are facing an uncertain future. Humans have collected too many of them for their shells and for their meat.

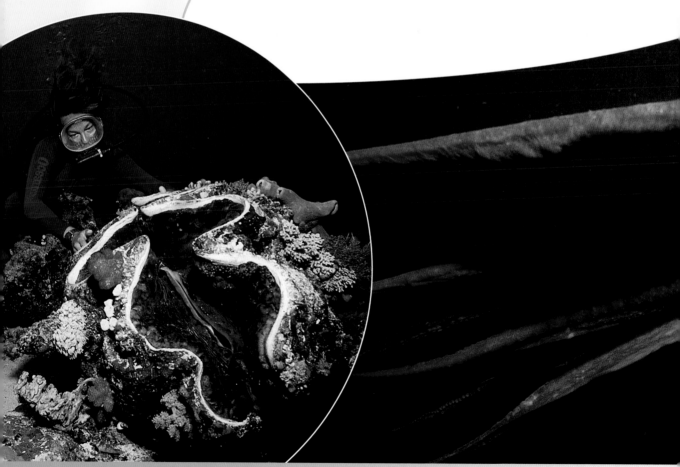

species type of living animal or plant

Massive molluscs

The largest known **bivalve** mollusc was a giant clam that weighed an amazing 333 kilograms (nearly 735 pounds), or as much as four adult humans!

Giant clams live in warm, shallow waters in the Pacific Ocean. Adult giant clams cannot move. They have to stay in the same place all their life. They suck in **plankton** to eat.

A useful shell

Humans have used giant clam shells for different purposes. This shell is being used to hold water for christenings.

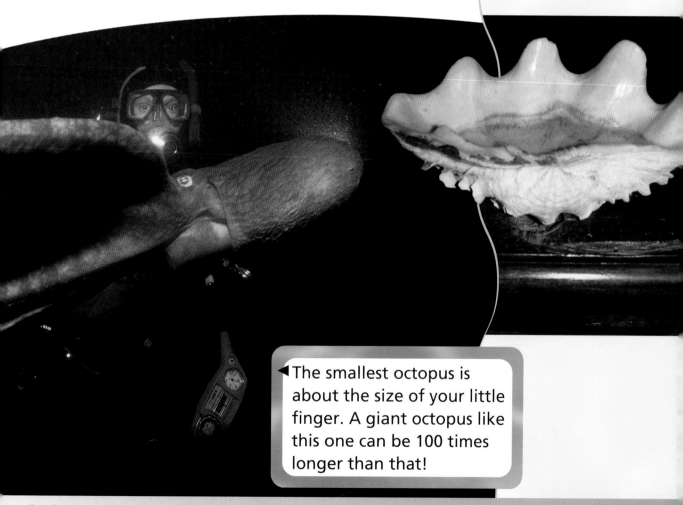

The smallest octopus is about the size of your little finger. A giant octopus like this one can be 100 times longer than that!

plankton tiny plants and animals that drift about in the sea

Giant squid

Far below the surface of the ocean lives an enormous mollusc that few people have seen alive. It is the giant squid.

▲ Sailors have sometimes seen fierce fights between sperm whales like this and giant squid.

Sometimes giant squid are washed up onto beaches. The largest was found on a New Zealand beach in 1887. Its **tentacles** were 18 metres (59 feet) long and its body was over 2 metres (6 feet) long!

Fight to the death

October 1966, Danger Point, South Africa. Two lighthouse keepers watched a young sperm whale being attacked by a giant squid. The squid finally won the fight and the whale was never seen again.

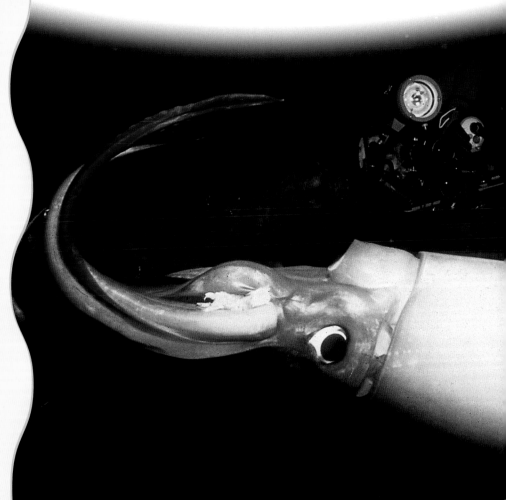

The mysterious giant

Giant squid live deep down in the ocean and do not usually come near the surface. This is why they are so mysterious and why we know so little about them.

In World War II, survivors from a sunken ship came across a giant squid. According to the story the squid attacked and ate one of them.

Tall stories?

A famous sea monster called the Kraken appears in old sea tales. It was huge and looked like a giant squid. It could sink ships by wrapping its tentacles around them and dragging them down.

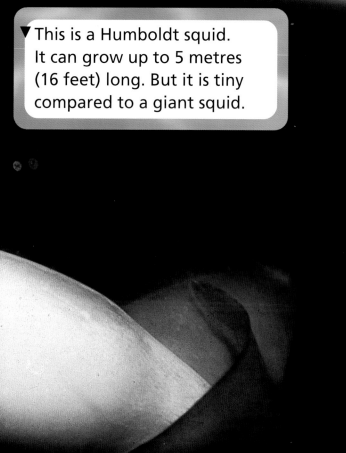

▼ This is a Humboldt squid. It can grow up to 5 metres (16 feet) long. But it is tiny compared to a giant squid.

Beautiful pearls

Pearls come in many colours – white, cream, pink, silver, gold, and even black. The older and bigger the pearl, the more valuable it is. Pearls with pinkish colours are the most valuable of all.

How to make a pearl

You may have heard that oysters can make pearls. But did you know that other water molluscs with shells make them too?

Sometimes **grit** gets into a mollusc shell. To make it smooth again, the mollusc coats it with **nacre**. Molluscs also use nacre to line their shells. Eventually the nacre-covered grit makes a pearl.

▼ It takes an oyster about two years to grow a pearl big enough to be used in jewellery.

grit very small piece of sand or stone

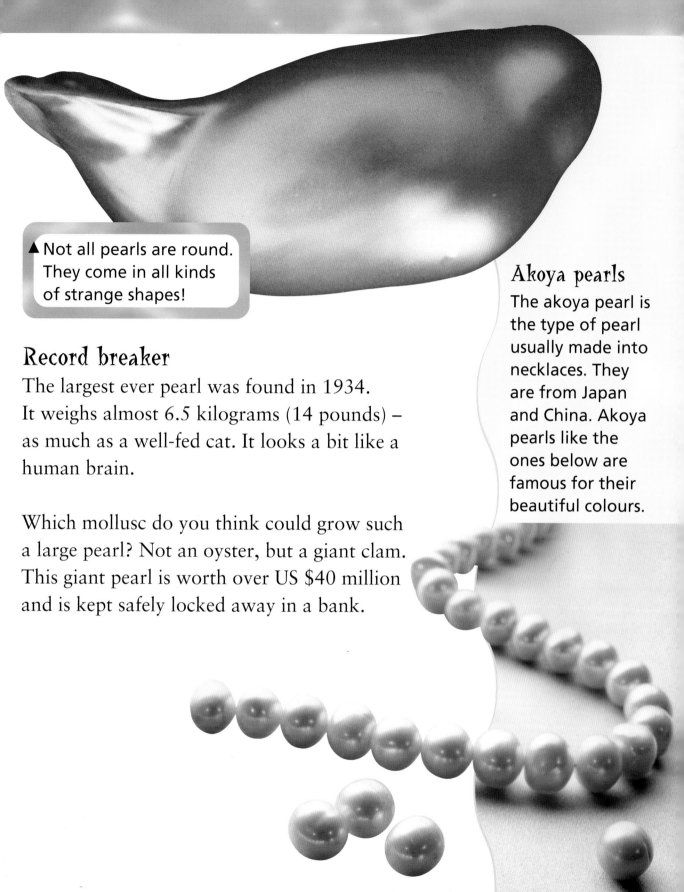

▲ Not all pearls are round. They come in all kinds of strange shapes!

Akoya pearls

The akoya pearl is the type of pearl usually made into necklaces. They are from Japan and China. Akoya pearls like the ones below are famous for their beautiful colours.

Record breaker

The largest ever pearl was found in 1934. It weighs almost 6.5 kilograms (14 pounds) – as much as a well-fed cat. It looks a bit like a human brain.

Which mollusc do you think could grow such a large pearl? Not an oyster, but a giant clam. This giant pearl is worth over US $40 million and is kept safely locked away in a bank.

nacre mother-of-pearl, a substance made by molluscs to coat the inside of their shells

Giant snails

The giant African snail comes from East Africa. It is tough and **breeds** fast. After **mating**, each partner lays eggs. These snails live for up to nine years. They can lay thousands of eggs during their lifetime.

In 1966, a boy returned to Miami in the USA with three of these snails as pets. He let them go. Seven years later the three snails had become 18,000 snails!

Giant sizes

Giant African land snails can reach 30 centimetres (12 inches) in length. Their shells are larger than a grapefruit.

Sea snails, such as this baler shell (above) are often even bigger in size.

mate when a male and female animal come together to produce young

Snail trouble

Although the giant African snail comes from Africa, it now lives in other countries, such as the USA and Australia.

This snail is a problem because it eats through farmers' **crops** really quickly. We have to keep it under control. Otherwise a lot of valuable food crops are at risk.

Greedy gobbler

Giant African snails eat cocoa, peanuts, rubber, beans, peas, and melons, as well as many other plants. This poster helps to make people aware of the dangers of this huge, hungry mollusc.

▼ This is the giant African snail. It is a big enemy of crop farmers.

Not All Alien Invaders Are From Outer Space

---

crop plant that humans grow for food, like wheat or potatoes

The wonderful world of slime

Have you seen squiggly white marks running up plant pots or across your garden? They are slime trails left by slugs and snails.

Slime is gooey and sticky. It is very useful for slugs and snails. Slime allows them to slide over grass and stones. It helps them climb trees, walls, and windows, and squeeze through small spaces.

Slimy friends

Banana slugs like this one **mate** in a thick goo of slime. It must taste delicious to the slugs, because they eat each other's slime before mating.

▶ Some gardeners use slug pellets to kill slugs. The slug shrivels up and dies. It leaves behind plenty of slime.

mate when a male and female animal come together to produce young

Squelchy!

When in danger, a slug oozes a coat of thick, slimy **mucus** from its body. The mucus makes the slug taste horrible to a **predator**. It also makes the slug very slippery to hold.

A coating of slime protects a slug's body and stops it from drying out. Salt is one thing slug slime cannot cope with. It makes a slug shrivel up and die.

Trails from snails

Snail's slime comes out from the front of their bodies. The snail can move over really sharp surfaces like thorns. It doesn't get hurt because the slime protects its body.

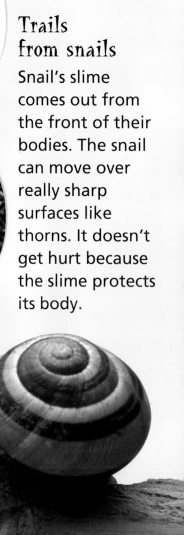

mucus slimy, slippery substance made by some animals

Endangered molluscs

Many animals are in danger of dying out in the world today. Sadly, some of them are molluscs.

Saving snails

Three **species** of Australian land snails are in danger of dying out. Since 1997 the Australian government has been trying to help the snails. They have made special laws that protect the places where these snails live.

On the edge

The dwarf wedge mussel is a small, yellowish-brown mussel. It lives in streams and rivers in North America.

Poisons used by farmers to protect their **crops** have entered the river water. These poisons have killed many of the mussels that lived there. The dwarf wedge mussel is now **endangered**.

▼This wood is in Australia. It is being carefully looked after to protect the snails that live in it.

endangered in danger of disappearing altogether

Queen conch

The queen conch can grow as long as your ruler (that's 30 centimetres, or 12 inches). It has a beautiful shell.

Today, there are very few queen conches left. Humans have caught too many of them for their meat and their attractive shells. Conch shells are often made into decorations for fishtanks and gardens.

▼ This mollusc shell has been made into a decoration.

Sandy snail

The sandbowl snail (below) is rare in the UK. It lives in sand dunes. People have built golf courses where it likes to live. This makes it difficult for the snail to find food or a safe home.

Molluscs matter

Molluscs are important to us and to life on Earth. We are still finding new **species** in the deep ocean. But we have a lot more to learn about molluscs and their amazing lives.

Molluscs and us

Molluscs can be harmful as well as helpful to us. They can damage ships and piers, and cause human diseases.

A disease called bilharzia affects 200 million people in hot countries. Water snails in these places are home to the **larvae** of a tiny worm. When people wash or paddle in rivers, the worm larvae get into their skin. The larvae then enter the blood and cause illness or even death.

▶ Scientists can find out more about molluscs by going deep down into the ocean in submarines like this.

larva (more than one are called larvae) young form of an animal that is very different from the adult

Molluscs and medicine

Molluscs are already used in medicine to help people. Ground-up oyster shells are used in **calcium** tablets to help us make strong bones and teeth.

Cone shells are deadly poisonous to humans. Their poison is a mixture of many different poisons. These affect different parts of the body, such as the nerves, muscles, and brain. Scientists can use these poisons to make medicine for people who are very ill or in pain.

Superglue!

Mussels make tiny threads to attach themselves to rocks. They are incredibly strong and sticky. Scientists think these threads could help us make a special superglue that is safe to use in hospitals.

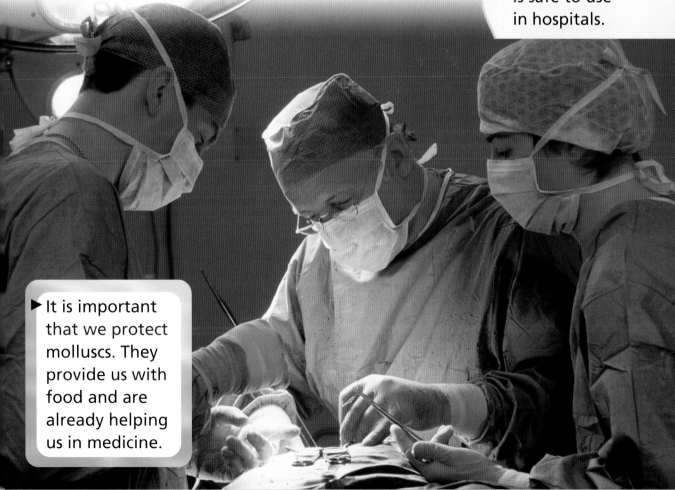

► It is important that we protect molluscs. They provide us with food and are already helping us in medicine.

calcium mineral that animals need in food for strong bones, teeth, or shells

Find out more

Websites
Wonders of the sea: molluscs
Website with photos and information about molluscs.
www.oceanic research.org/ mollusk.html

The Cephalopod Page
Website with photos and information about octopuses, squid, and cuttlefish.
http://www.dal. ca/~ceph/TCP/

The Learning Zone
Website with pictures, information, and quizzes on molluscs.
www.oum.ox.ac. uk/children/fossils /molluscs.htm

Books
Gentle Giant Octopus (Read and Wonder), Karen Wallace (Walker, 2002)
Minibeasts: Slugs and Snails, Claire Llewellyn (Franklin Watts, 2002)
Variety of Life: Molluscs, Joy Richardson (Franklin Watts, 2003)

World wide web
To find out more about molluscs you can search the Internet. Use keywords like these:
• "giant African snail"
• pearl +oyster
• "blue-ringed octopus"
You can find your own keywords by using words from this book. The search tips on page 53 will help you find useful websites.

Search tips

There are billions of pages on the Internet. It can be difficult to find exactly what you are looking for. These tips will help you find useful websites more quickly:

- Know what you want to find out about
- Use simple keywords
- Use two to six keywords in a search
- Only use names of people, places, or things
- Put double quote marks around words that go together, for example "sea slug"

Where to search

Search engine

A search engine looks through millions of website pages. It lists all the sites that match the words in the search box. You will find the best matches are at the top of the list, on the first page.

Search directory

A person instead of a computer has sorted a search directory. You can search by keyword or subject and browse through the different sites. It is like looking through books on a library shelf.

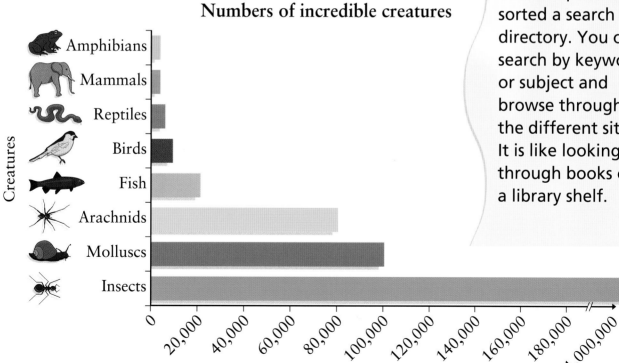

Numbers of incredible creatures

Creatures: Amphibians, Mammals, Reptiles, Birds, Fish, Arachnids, Molluscs, Insects

Number of species (approximate)

Glossary

algae type of plant without stems that grows in water or on rocks

bivalve mollusc with two shells joined at a hinge

breed produce young

calcium mineral that animals need in food for strong bones, teeth, or shells

carnivore animal that eats meat

cephalopod ('sef-a-la-pod') mollusc that has tentacles around its mouth

chiton ('ky-ton') mollusc with an oval shell made up of eight overlapping plates

cockle sea mollusc that has a ribbed bivalve shell

coral tiny sea animals that use rings of tentacles for feeding. Many have hard outer bodies.

crop plant that humans grow for food, like wheat or potatoes

endangered in danger of disappearing altogether

gastropod mollusc that moves along on its soft belly

gills delicate, feathery structures that allow some animals to breathe under water

grit very small piece of sand or stone

herbivore animal that eats only plants – a vegetarian

hinge joint that moves, like the part that fixes a door to a frame and allows it to open and close

invertebrate animal without a backbone

larva (more than one are called larvae) young form of an animal that is very different from the adult

mate when a male and female animal come together to produce young

mimic (noun) one living thing that can copy another living thing

mucus slimy, slippery substance made by some animals

muscular has strong muscles

nacre mother-of-pearl, a substance made by molluscs to coat the inside of their shells

nutrient substance found in food that is needed by the body to grow strong and healthy

oxygen one of the gases in air and water that all living things need

parasite animal or plant that lives in or on another living thing

plankton tiny plants and animals that drift about in the sea

predator animal that kills and eats other animals

prey animal that is killed and eaten by other animals

radula tongue that is long and rough

scallop bivalve mollusc that has semicircular shells with wavy edges

species type of living animal or plant

survive stay alive despite danger and difficulties

tentacle part of an animal that looks like a long, thin, bendy arm

whelk kind of large sea snail

Index

Titles in the *Freestyle Express*: *Incredible Creatures* series include:

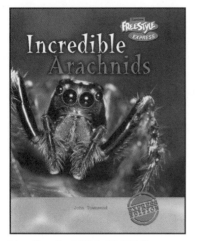

Hardback: 1844 434516

Hardback: 1844 434524

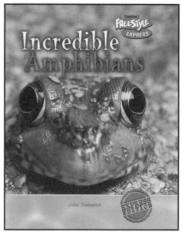

Hardback: 1844 434532

Hardback: 1844 434540

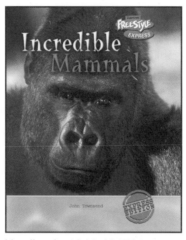

Hardback: 1844 434761

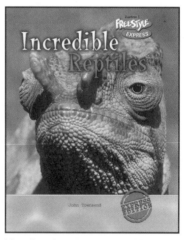

Hardback: 1844 43477X

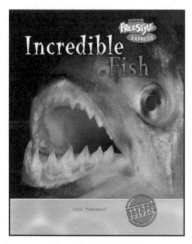

Hardback: 1844 435172

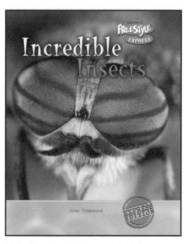

Hardback: 1844 435180

Find out about other Freestyle Express titles on our website www.raintreepublishers.co.uk